THE SCHOOL OF LIFE is dedicated to exploring life's big questions: *How can we fulfil our potential? Can work be inspiring? Why does community matter? Can relationships last a lifetime?* We don't have all the answers, but we will direct you towards a variety of useful ideas – from philosophy to literature, psychology to the visual arts – that are guaranteed to stimulate, provoke, nourish and console.

THESCHOOLOFLIFE.COM

By the same author:

Conditions of Love
How to Worry Less About Money
In Search of Civilization
Love, Life, Goethe
The Secret Power of Beauty

By Friedrich Nietzsche:

Beyond Good and Evil
David Strauss, the Confessor and the Writer
Human, All Too Human
On the Genealogy of Morality
On the Uses and Disadvantages of History for Life
Richard Wagner in Bayreuth
Schopenhauer as Educator
The Birth of Tragedy
The Case of Wagner
The Gay Science
Twilight of the Idols

NIETZSCHE

Great Thinkers on Modern Life

John Armstrong

PEGASUS BOOKS
NEW YORK LONDON

NIETZSCHE

Pegasus Books LLC
80 Broad Street, 5th Floor
New York, NY 10004

First Pegasus Books edition 2015

ISBN: 978-1-60598-675-3

10 9 8 7 8 6 5 4 3 2 1

Printed in the United States of America
Distributed by W. W. Norton & Company, Inc.

CONTENTS

INTRODUCTION

....

No one is born with the ability to say 'Nietzsche'.
One way is to remember that Nietzsche rhymes with
'teach ya' – as memorably demonstrated in Monty
Python's philosophers' drinking song.

Friedrich Nietzsche (1844–1900) was one of the most
daring and ambitious thinkers of the nineteenth
century. He felt that the prevailing values of his society
were obstacles to the good life and launched a one-man
revolution to transform pretty much everything. He
particularly relished attacking what he regarded as
conventional pieties or reversing our expectations: he
decides, for example, that pity might not always be a
good thing or that loneliness is good for us. He likes
taking risks and he's not afraid of shocking us.

Nietzsche was born into a deeply religious family
(his father, uncle and grandfather were all pastors). He
was an extremely conscientious schoolboy and student,
especially good at Greek. He so impressed his teachers
that in his mid-twenties he was appointed professor of
classics at the small University of Basle.

Around the age of twenty he lost his religious faith, arriving at the conclusion that there was no adequate evidence for the existence of God. He became, in some ways, deeply hostile to Christianity. In fact, he seems to have been irritated by almost every aspect of German culture as it then was. But although he was shy and lacking in self-confidence, Nietzsche was filled with a longing to speak intently into the lives of others and to help them in their deepest spiritual needs.

Just as his academic career was taking off he became close friends with Germany's foremost cultural figure, the composer Richard Wagner. Wagner wanted to transform the imaginative life of Europe and Nietzsche was fired with equally grand ideas. He soon felt constrained by the careful, cautious limits of academic life.

In 1870 (when Nietzsche was twenty-six) the recently unified, rapidly industrializing Germany waged a very successful war against France. Nietzsche served as a medical orderly. Under the strategic leadership of Bismarck, Germany entered a period of immense self-confidence and collective pride. This was extremely upsetting to Nietzsche. All his dislike and frustration and contempt for the people around him seemed defeated by their all too obvious material and political triumphs. It's very hard to get much response when you criticize people who think themselves amazingly successful.

In 1879, after a few years of teaching at Basle, Nietzsche retired on a small pension paid by the university. His health was precarious. He spent much time in Italy and Switzerland, often in small towns, living quietly and alone. He broke with Wagner and came to see his former mentor as a symptom of the very spiritual sickness that needed curing.

For a while Nietzsche thought of marriage and family life, but he felt terribly betrayed in his closest relationships with women. His craving for ideal friendship was unsatisfied. But, crucially, he did not repudiate the things he wanted simply because he was unable to attain them himself.

All his life, even though he was single, he believed that marriage could be wonderful. He also believed, despite his lack of both, that power and fame were tremendous honours and great resources. He held good health in the highest esteem, as central to the good life, even though he was frequently ill. He believed in the value of a life of action, despite being cooped up in small lodgings, poring over his books. He asserted the importance of strong, healthy instincts, which he regarded as far more important than his own special skill – the acquisition of scholarly knowledge.

Living often alone, in poor health, short of money, Nietzsche wrote a sequence of books that have made him one of the founding figures of the modern world of ideas. But at the time few were paying attention, and he was deeply wounded by the lack of interest his contemporaries showed in his ideas. But somehow he 'overcame' this, to use one of his favourite terms. Instead of giving up he devoted incredible energy and fertility of mind to the elaboration of views that for many years mattered only to him.

In 1889 while he was living in Turin, delighting in the golden autumnal weather and going repeatedly to the opera house to hear performances of Bizet's *Carmen*, he saw a horse being beaten by its driver. He rushed towards the horse shouting: 'I understand, I understand.' He then collapsed and was taken back to his inn.

For the rest of his life he was in the grip of intense delusions. He was sent back to Germany to live with his sister whom he had disliked and distrusted. She established him as a 'seer' – he grew a long white beard and sat robed in a white toga. She and her husband edited Nietzsche's works so as to align them with German Nationalism and the glorification of military power, grotesquely distorting his clearest intentions. Nietzsche loathed all groups; he was entirely devoted to cultivating the strength and wisdom of individuals.

While suffering from pneumonia he died of a stroke at the end of August 1900.

Trying to do the impossible and sum up his life's work in a single phrase, Nietzsche said that he wanted to bring about the 're-evaluation of all values'. It's a striking phrase. But what does it mean?

Nietzsche believed that values are the central concern in life: What do you love? What do you think is important? What do you give priority to? What do you take seriously in your life and what do you brush aside as irrelevant? This is not just a matter of what you say or what you tell yourself that you believe. It is played out in conduct, habit and choices. Someone may say that they care about global justice, but in their day-to-day life this does not actually take centre stage. Values should be lived out in our lives and should shape every aspect of our existence.

Nietzsche thought that the people he lived amongst mostly had the wrong values. They cared about the wrong things and for the wrong reasons.

But what are the right values to have? Through his works, Nietzsche offers us a series of lessons on what he thinks our true concerns should be and what we should hold in high esteem. In other words, he offers lessons for life.

1

HOW TO FIND
YOUR BEST SELF

....

Sometimes we feel frustrated with 'who we are'. We yearn to be better than we are. But we are not quite sure what this means.

Nietzsche is very sympathetic to this kind of restlessness. He doesn't chide us to count our blessings and remember that things could be a lot worse; or say that in the overall condition of the world we count ourselves as terribly lucky, and that we should pull ourselves together. Instead he invites us to get interested in what is going on when we feel dissatisfied with ourselves. He sees this as a sign of good psychological health. He wants us to get to know this dissatisfaction, take it seriously and do something about it.

Some first shots at imagining a better version of oneself might be: make more money, do more exciting things, get a job you love, move house, find an exit from an unsatisfactory relationship, make some new friends, get a masters degree. These could be very good goals. But notice that they are all external. They are about things we could do or have. What about what it is like to be us: who are we really, in and of ourselves? And why don't we set about it? Why don't we become the people we want to be? Are we too lazy?

This is the question Nietzsche asks in an essay called *Schopenhauer as Educator.*

A traveller, who had seen many countries, was asked what common attribute he had found among people. He answered: 'They have a tendency to sloth.'

Many may think that the fuller truth would have been: 'They are all timid.' They hide themselves behind 'manners' and 'opinions'.

At bottom every man knows that he is a unique being, the like of which can appear only once on this earth. By no extraordinary chance will such a marvellous piece of diversity in unity, as he is, ever be put together a second time. He knows this, but hides it like a guilty secret. Why? From fear of his neighbour, who looks only for the latest convention-alities in him, and is wrapped up in them himself.

But what is it that forces the man to fear his neighbour, to think and act with his herd, and not seek his own joy?

Shyness, perhaps, in a few rare cases. But in the majority it is idleness – taking things easily. In a word, the 'tendency to sloth', of which the traveller spoke. He was right. People are more slothful than timid. Their greatest fear is the heavy burden that uncompromising honesty and nakedness of speech and action would lay on them.

It is only artists who hate this lazy wandering in borrowed manners and ill-fitting opinions. They discover the guilty secret of the bad conscience: the disowned truth that each human being is a unique marvel.

Artists show us how, even in every little movement of the muscles, a man is an individual self. And further – as an analytical deduction from his individuality – a beautiful and interesting object: a new and incredible phenomenon (as is every work of nature) that can never become tedious.

If a great thinker despises people, it is because they are lazy; they seem like broken bits of crockery, not worth mending.

The man who does not want to remain in the general mass, has only to stop 'taking things easy'. He needs to follow his conscience, which cries out: 'Be yourself! The way you behave and think and desire at the moment – this is not you!'

Every youthful soul hears this cry day and night, and thrills to hear it. The soul guesses at a special quota of happiness that has been from eternity destined for it – if only it can find help to get there. But you cannot be helped towards your true happiness so long as you are bound by the chains of Opinion and of Fear.

And how comfortless and unmeaning life is without this deliverance! There is no more desolate or outcast creature in nature than the man who has broken away from his true genius and does nothing but peer aimlessly about.

There is no reason to attack, or criticize, such a man. He is a husk without a kernel; a painted cloth, tattered and sagging; a scarecrow ghost, that can rouse no fear, and certainly no pity.

The sluggard 'kills time'. But an era that looks for salvation in public opinion – that is, in private laziness – should itself be 'killed', once and for all.

I mean that it will be blotted from life's true History of Liberty. Later generations will be greatly disgusted, when they look back at a period ruled by shadow-men projected on the screen of public opinion. To some far posterity our age may well be the darkest chapter of history, the most unknown because the least human.

I have walked through the new streets of our cities, and thought how of all the dreadful houses that these gentlemen with their public opinion have built for themselves not a stone will remain in a hundred years. And the opinions of these busy masons may well have fallen along with the buildings.

Yet how full of hope should anyone be who feels they are not a citizen of this age! If they were a citizen, they would have to help with the work of 'killing their time', and they would – as citizens – perish with it. But someone who does not feel a citizen of this age might wish instead to bring to life a better time, and in that life themselves to live.

But even if the future offers us nothing to hope for, the wonderful fact of our existing at this present moment of time gives us the greatest encouragement to live after our own rule and measure. It is inexplicable that we should be living just today, though there has been an infinity of time in which we might have existed. We own nothing but a span's length (a 'today') in this infinity; we must reveal why we exist.

We have to answer for our existence to ourselves and will therefore be our own true pilots, and not admit that our existence is random or pointless.

One must take a bold and reckless way with the riddle [of life]; especially as the key is apt to be lost, however things turn out.

Why cling to your bit of earth, or your little business, or listen to what your neighbour says? It is so provincial to bind oneself to views which are no longer binding a couple of hundred miles away. East and West are signs that somebody chalks up to fool cowards like us.

'I will make the attempt to gain freedom,' says the youthful soul; 'and will be hindered, just because two nations happen to hate each other and go to war, or because there is a sea between two parts of the earth, or a religion is taught in the vicinity, which did not exist two thousand years ago.

'And this is not – you,' the soul says. 'No one can build the bridge, over which you must cross the river of life, except you alone. There are paths and bridges and demi-gods without number, that will gladly carry you over, but only at the price of losing your own self: your self would have to be mortgaged, and then lost.

'There is one road along which no one can go, except you. Do not ask where it leads; go forward. Who was it that spoke these true words: "A man never rises higher than when he does not know where his road will take him"?'

How can we 'find ourselves' again? How can man 'know himself'? He is a thing obscure and veiled. If the hare has seven skins, man can cast from him seventy times seven skins, and not be able to say: 'Here you truly are; this is skin no more.'

Also this digging into one's self, this straight, violent descent into the pit of one's being, is a troublesome and dangerous business to start. You may easily take such hurt, that no doctor can heal you. And what is the point: since everything bears witness to our essence – our friendships and enmities, our looks and greetings, our memories and forgetfulnesses, our books and our writing!

This is the most effective way: let the growing soul look at life with the question: 'What have you truly loved? What has drawn you upward, mastered and blessed you?'

Set up the things that you have honoured in front of you. Maybe they will reveal, in their being and their order, a law which is the fundamental law of your own self.

Compare these objects. Consider how one of them completes and broadens and transcends and explains another: how they form a ladder which all the time you have been climbing to find your true self.

For your true self does not lie deeply hidden *within* you. It is at an infinite height *above* you – at least, above what you commonly take to be yourself.

(*Schopenhauer as Educator*, 1874)

He sums it up by defining education:

Real education is a liberation. It removes the weeds and rubbish and vermin that attack the delicate shoots of the plant. Real education is the light warmth and tender rain.

(*Schopenhauer as Educator*, 1874)

What is this experience of finding something 'higher' or 'above' ourselves? One way of taking this is to think of people we admire. People who seem, in some way, to already be the kind of person we want to become. It's not just that we admire them for their achievements

– as we might admire a great athlete or explorer or successful entrepreneur. It's rather that there is something about this person's way of being, their attitudes, their manner of existing, that speaks to us and entices us – and hints at our own good development.

Nietzsche was most deeply impressed by the great German poet (and dramatist, civil servant, traveller, lover, collector, diplomat, dramatist, novelist . . .) Goethe:

> *Goethe* – not a German event but a European one: a grand attempt to return to overcome the eighteenth century [Goethe's own times] through a return to nature, through a going-*up* to the naturalness of the Renaissance, a kind of self-over-coming on the part of that century. – He bore within him its strongest instincts: sentimentality, nature-idolatry, the anti-historical, the idealistic, the unreal and revolutionary (– the last is only a form of the unreal). He called to his aid history, the natural sciences, antiquity, likewise Spinoza, above all practical activity; he surrounded himself with nothing but closed horizons; he did not sever himself from life, he placed himself within it; nothing could discourage him and he took as much as possible upon himself, above himself, within himself. What he aspired to was *totality*; he strove against the separation of reason, sensuality, feeling, will; he disciplined himself to a whole; he *created* himself . . .

Goethe conceived of a strong, highly cultured human being, skilled in all physical accomplishments, who, keeping himself in check and having reverence for himself, dares to allow himself the whole compass and wealth of naturalness, who is strong enough for this freedom; a man of tolerance, not out of weakness, but out of strength, because he knows how to employ to his advantage what would destroy an average nature; a man to whom nothing is forbidden, except it be *weakness*, whether that virtue be called vice or virtue . . .

A spirit thus *emancipated* stands in the midst of the universe with a joyful and trusting fatalism, in the *faith* that only what is separate and individual may be rejected, that in the totality everything is redeemed and affirmed – *he no longer denies* . . .

(*Twilight of the Idols*, 1889)

The person you admire stands 'above' you – and excites admiration, and perhaps at times envy.

Nietzsche is not just looking at his hero with wordless admiration, or applause. He wants to fathom Goethe's secret. He wants to know *how* that admirable man became the person he was. This is the key question: How are the impressive things actually accomplished? It's not enough just to look on. We want to become more like the things we admire.

Worshipping the genius out of vanity. Because we think well of ourselves, but in no way expect that we could ever make the preparatory sketch for a painting by Raphael or a scene like one in a play by Shakespeare, we convince ourselves that the ability to do so is quite excessively wonderful, a quite uncommon accident, or, if we still have a religious sensibility, a grace from above. Thus our vanity, our self-love, furthers the worship of the genius, for it does not hurt only if we think of it as very remote from ourselves, as a miracle (Goethe, who was without envy, called Shakespeare his 'star of the furthest height', recalling to us that line 'one does not covet the stars').

But those insinuations of our vanity aside, the activity of the genius seems in no way fundamentally different from the activity of a mechanical inventor, a scholar of astronomy or history, a master tactician. All these activities are explained when one imagines men whose thinking is active in one particular direction; who use everything to that end; who always observe eagerly their inner life and that of other people; who see models, stimulation everywhere; who do not tire of rearranging their material.

The genius, too, does nothing other than first learn to place stones, then to build, always seeking material, always forming and reforming it. Every human activity is amazingly complicated, not only that of the genius: but none is a 'miracle'.

From where, then, the belief that there is genius only in the artist, orator or philosopher? That only they have 'intuition' (thus attributing to them a kind of magical eye glass by which they can see directly into 'being')? It is evident that people speak of genius only where they find the effects of the great intellect most agreeable and, on the other hand, where they do not want to feel envy. To call someone 'divine' means 'Here we do not have to compete.' Furthermore, everything that is complete and perfect is admired; everything evolved is underestimated. Now, no one can see in an artist's work *how* it evolved: that is its advantage, for wherever we can see the evolution we grow somewhat cooler.

(*Human, All Too Human*, 1878)

But to 'grow cooler' is, really, a good thing. Because what it does is bring us closer to the sense that we too have it in our power to reach after great things. But not – as we formerly imagined – by some magnificent act of accomplishment. Rather by concentration of our efforts, slow mastery, the gradual accumulation of relevant insights, the painstaking sorting out of what is crucial from what is misleading, by practice and repetition.

Paradoxical as it might sound, Nietzsche warns that such recognition is heard as bad news. For if the great things are doable then, indeed, we can compete. The great work is no longer 'divine'. It is no longer cast as something impossibly distant.

In essence, what Nietzsche is saying is this: the things we long to do and accomplish – the kind of person we might hope to become – are in fact within reach. But the path to each of those goals has this difficulty to it: it is a path that involves suffering, annoyance with oneself, disappointment, envy and frustration. He is saying that it is always through such pains that good things emerge. They do not occur as matters of spontaneous luck. Looking on from the outside at what we admire (a successful person) we see the effect. But we do not usually also get the chance to closely observe the evolutionary history. We don't see the nights of anguish, the fears, the insecurity. Such insight, however, is strangely heartening. It helps us see that suffering is not a sign of failing to be the best version of oneself, but a necessary part of the process of becoming who we want to – and should – be.

2

ON VISITING
THE PYRAMIDS

....

Life presents us with many fascinating and exciting things, such as seeing the Pyramids (or going to a play, or sitting next to someone interesting at dinner, or reading a biography . . .)

But too often the experience does not really stick. We enjoy it, but it does not change us. It does not have a deep or lasting effect. Normally we don't mind too much – this is the very familiar pattern of life. But maybe we should mind more. Nietzsche suggests that we should take these opportunities very seriously. And he thinks that we don't get the best out of them because we don't ask a key question: what is this experience for – what actually do we want from it, where do we think it should contribute to our lives?

He looks at the whole topic of history and asks what is history for. It feels like a very odd question. We don't normally ask such a basic question about grand things like history. We usually reserve it for simpler encounters: looking at the dashboard of someone's car and asking 'what's that button for?'

The fact that life does need the service of history must be as clearly grasped as that an excess of history hurts it; this will be proved later. History is necessary to the living man in relation to three different areas: his action and struggle, his conservatism and reverence, his suffering and his desire for deliverance.

These three relations answer to the three kinds of history – so far as they can be distinguished – the monumental, the antiquarian and the critical.

History is necessary above all to the man of action and power who fights a great fight and needs examples, teachers and comforters; he cannot find them among his contemporaries. It was necessary in this sense to poet, philosopher and playwright Friedrich Schiller; for our time is so evil, Goethe says, that the poet meets no nature that will profit him among living men. The ancient Greek historian Polybius is thinking of the active man when he calls political history the true preparation for governing a state: it is the great teacher that shows us how to bear steadfastly the reverses of fortune, by reminding us of what others have suffered. Whoever has learned to recognize this meaning in history must hate to see curious tourists and laborious beetle-hunters climbing up the great pyramids of antiquity. He does not wish to meet the idler who is rushing through the picture-galleries of the past for a new distraction or sensation, where he himself is looking for instruction and encouragement. To avoid being troubled by the weak and hopeless idlers, and those whose apparent activity is merely neurotic, he looks behind him and stays his course towards the goal in order to breathe. His goal perhaps is his own, but often it is the nation's, or humanity's at large: he avoids quietism, and uses history as a weapon against it. For the most part he has no hope of reward except fame, which means the expectation of a niche in the temple of history, where he in his turn may be the consoler and counsellor of posterity. For he sees that what has once been able to extend the conception 'man' and give it a fairer content – and better meaning – must ever exist for the same purpose and task.

The great moments in the individual battle to enrich the nature of humanity form a chain, a high road for humanity through the ages, and the highest points of those vanished moments are yet great and living for men; and this is the fundamental idea of the belief in humanity, that finds a voice in the demand for a 'monumental history'.

But the fiercest battle is fought around the demand for greatness to be eternal. Every other living thing cries no. 'Away with the monuments,' is the watchword. Dull custom fills all the chambers of the world with its meanness, and rises in thick vapour around anything that is great, barring its way to immortality, blinding and stifling it. And the way passes through mortal brains! Through the brains of sick and short-lived beasts that ever rise to the surface to breathe, and painfully keep off annihilation for a little space. For they wish but one thing: to live at any cost. Who would ever dream of any 'monumental history' – the hard torch-race that alone gives life to greatness – among them? And yet there are always men awakening, who are strengthened and made happy by gazing on past greatness, as though man's life were a lordly thing; and the fairest fruit of this bitter tree is the knowledge that there was once a man who walked sternly and proudly through this world, another who had pity and loving-kindness, another who lived in contemplation – but all leaving one truth behind them, that his life is the fairest who thinks least about immediate advantage in life. The common man snatches greedily at this little span, with tragic earnestness, but they, on their way to monumental history and immortality, knew how to greet it with Olympic laughter, or at least with a lofty scorn, and they went down to their graves in irony – for what had they to bury ? Only what they had always treated as dross, refuse and vanity, and which now falls into its true home of oblivion, after being so long the sport of their contempt.

One thing will live – the sign-manual of their inmost being, the rare flash of light, the deed, the creation

– because posterity cannot do without it. In this spiritualized form fame is something more than 'the sweetest morsel for our egoism' – in Schopenhauer's phrase – it is the belief in the oneness and continuity of the great in every age, and a protest against the change and decay of generations.

What is the use to the modern man of this 'monumental' contemplation of the past, this preoccupation with the rare and classic? It is the knowledge that the great thing existed and was therefore possible, and so may be possible again. He is heartened on his way; for his doubt in weaker moments, whether his desire be not for the impossible, is struck aside.

Suppose one believes that no more than a hundred men, brought up in the new spirit, efficient and productive, were needed to give the death-blow to the present fashion of education in Germany; he will gather strength from the remembrance that the culture of the Renaissance was raised on the shoulders of such another band of a hundred men. And yet if we really wish to learn something from an example, how vague and elusive do we find the comparison! If it is to give us strength, many of the differences must be neglected, the individuality of the past forced into a general formula and all the sharp angles broken off for the sake of correspondence.

As long as the soul of history is found in the great impulse that it gives to a powerful spirit, as long as the past is principally used as a model for imitation, it is always in danger of being a little altered and touched up, and brought nearer to fiction. So as to speak more powerfully to us. Sometimes there is no possible distinction between a 'monumental' past and a mythical romance, as the same motives for action can be gathered from the one world as the other. If this monumental method of surveying the past dominates the others – the antiquarian and the critical, which I shall shortly describe – the past itself suffers wrong.

(On the Uses and Disadvantages of History for Life, 1874)

The key question is: what do we need from the things we encounter? What are we trying to do with them? Nietzsche is a great fighter in the war on randomness.

It's not that our purposes always have to be tremendously elevated. The point is that we need to have some view of what we want. Nietzsche is getting us to see how often we drift idly around the important and great things that we encounter. We don't ask much of them. We don't ask them to guide our lives, or inspire us, or comfort us. We consider them interesting – and then don't imagine that they have anything important to say to us about ourselves.

Secondly, history is necessary to the man of conservative and reverent nature, who looks back to the origins of his existence with love and trust; through it, he gives thanks for life. He is careful to preserve what survives from ancient days, and will reproduce the conditions of his own upbringing for those who come after him; thus he does life a service. The possession of his ancestors' furniture changes its meaning in his soul: for his soul is rather possessed by it. All that is small and limited, mouldy and obsolete, gains a worth and inviolability of its own from the conservative and reverent soul of the antiquary migrating into it, and building a secret nest there. The history of his town becomes the history of himself; he looks on the walls, the turreted gate, the town council, the fair, as an illustrated diary of his youth, and sees himself in it all – his strength, industry, desire, reason, faults and follies. 'Here one could live,' he says, 'as one can live here now – and will go on living; for we are tough folk, and will not be uprooted in the night.' And so, with his 'we', he surveys the marvellous individual life of the past and identifies himself with the spirit of the house, the family and the city. He greets the soul of his people from afar as his own, across the dim and troubled centuries.

. . .

But the greatest value of this antiquarian spirit of reverence lies in the simple emotions of pleasure and content that it lends to the drab, rough, even painful circumstances of a nation's or individual's life: the celebrated historian Niebuhr confesses that he could live happily on a moor among free peasants with a history, and would never feel the want of art. How could history serve life better than by anchoring the less gifted types of people to the homes and customs of their ancestors, and keeping them from ranging far afield in search of better, to find only struggle and competition? The influence that ties men down to the same companions and circumstances, to the daily round of toil, to their bare mountainside – seems to be selfish and unreasonable: but it is a healthy unreason and of profit to the community; as everyone knows who has clearly realized the terrible consequences of mere desire for migration and adventure – perhaps in whole peoples – or who watches the destiny of a nation that has lost confidence in its earlier days, and is given up to a restless cosmopolitanism and an unceasing desire for novelty. The feeling of the tree that clings to its roots, the happiness of knowing one's growth to be not merely arbitrary and fortuitous, but the inheritance, the fruit and blossom of a past, that does not merely justify but crown the present – this is what we nowadays prefer to call the real historical sense.

. . .

There is always the danger (in this approach) that whatever happens to be ancient will be regarded as equally venerable, and everything that is left out of this respect for antiquity, like a new spirit, will be rejected as an enemy. The Greeks themselves admitted the archaic style of plastic art by the side of the freer and greater style; and later, did not merely tolerate the pointed nose and the cold mouth, but made them even a canon of taste. If the judgement of a people harden in this way, and history's service to the past life be to undermine a further and higher life; if the historical sense no longer preserve life, but mummify it: then the tree dies, unnaturally, from the top downwards, and at last the roots themselves wither.

Antiquarian history degenerates from the moment that it no longer gives a soul and inspiration to the fresh life of the present. The spring of piety is dried up, but the learned habit persists without it and revolves complacently round its own centre. The horrid spectacle is seen of the mad collector raking over all the dust-heaps of the past. He breathes a mouldy air; the antiquarian habit may degrade a considerable talent, a real spiritual need in him, to a mere insatiable curiosity for everything old: he often sinks so low as to be satisfied with any food, and greedily devour all the scraps that fall from the bibliographical table.

(On the Uses and Disadvantages of History for Life, 1874)

The danger here is that while the piety may wither away, the attitude of scholarly devotion – the preoccupation with every little detail – will continue – in which case the effort no longer serves any good living purpose. It is no longer something that makes us larger and stronger. Instead it becomes a retreat from life; a preoccupation that gets in the way of us working out what we actually care about and want and need.

Are you oppressed by a present trouble, which you need history to help you throw off?

Man must have the strength to break up the past; and apply it too, in order to live. He must bring the past to the bar of judgement, interrogate it remorse-lessly, and finally condemn it. Every past is worth condemning: this is the rule in mortal affairs, which always contain a large measure of human power and human weakness. It is not justice that sits in judge-ment here; nor mercy that proclaims the verdict; but only the dim, driving force that insatiably desires – itself. Its sentence is always unmerciful, always unjust, as it never flows from a pure fountain of knowledge: though it would generally turn out the same, if Justice herself delivered it. 'For everything that is born is worthy of being destroyed: better were it then that nothing should be born.' It requires great strength to be able to live and forget how far life and injustice are one. Luther himself once said that the world only arose by an oversight of God; if he had ever dreamed of heavy artillery he would never have created it. The same life that needs forgetfulness, needs sometimes its destruction; for should the injustice of something ever become obvious – a monopoly, a caste, a dynasty for example – the thing deserves to fall. Its past is critically examined, the knife put to its roots, and all the 'pieties' are grimly trodden underfoot.

For as we are merely the result of previous generations we are also the result of their errors, passions, and crimes: it is impossible to shake off this chain. Though we condemn the errors and think we have escaped them, we cannot escape the fact that we spring from them. At best, it comes to a conflict between our innate, inherited nature and our knowledge, between a stern, new discipline and an ancient tradition; and we plant a new way of life, a new instinct, a second nature, that withers the first.

(On the Uses and Disadvantages of History for Life, 1874)

The danger here is that we may wield the terrible condemning power of critical history to no great effect. As Nietzsche sees it, this ought to be the opening move in the creation of a new and better order of things. We cast off the past in order to bring in something genuinely better – and because we have an urgent need of doing this. But we can become slaves of a critical habit. We look at the past and condemn, not because we have any great need to do so, not because this really is crucial in creating the future we want, but because we have no particular sense of what we want from the past and we condemn it as a kind of prejudicial sport – much as bigots condemn anything that is unfamiliar or alien to them.

This is how history can serve life. Every man and nation needs a certain knowledge of the past, whether it be through monumental, antiquarian or critical history, according to his objects, powers and necessities. The need is not that of the mere thinkers who only look on at life, or the few who desire knowledge and can only be satisfied with knowledge; but it has always a reference to the purpose of life, and is under its absolute rule and direction. This is the natural relation of an age, a culture and a people to history; hunger is its source, necessity its norm, the inner plastic power assigns its limits. The knowledge of the past is only desired for the service of the future and the present, not to weaken the present or undermine a living future.

(*On the Uses and Disadvantages
of History for Life*, 1874)

Nietzsche wants us to think of history as a kind of therapy, as offering us help to become the kind of people we want to be. But we have to diagnose our own needs before we can seek out the right kind of help.

Are you trying to undertake a great task with which you need help – help to remain cheerful and confident in the face of great difficulties? Are you by nature a pious person? Do you revere and love certain things in the past because they seem to be part of yourself?

We should pay a great deal more attention to purpose than we normally do. We tend not to ask: What is my visit to the Pyramids (or the Eiffel Tower, or the Tate Modern) actually for? That is, what true need of mine does it serve? It's not enough to say: 'I want to see these things with my own eyes,' or 'It's on my bucket list,' or 'It's famous.' These 'reasons' do not latch onto genuine needs. Nietzsche is asking us to regard our lives as more precious – our attention and devotion are commodities that are in short supply, valuable resources that should not be wasted.

3

DEALING WITH
CONFLICT

....

We are not completely consistent creatures. There might be a sensible, responsible part of yourself, and a carefree, cavalier aspect. In some ways you might be deeply loyal and conservative in your attitudes to relationships – and at the same time yearn for adventure and experimentation.

A natural response might be to try to eliminate this conflict by suppressing one set of demands (talking ourselves out of them), being more controlled.

Nietzsche wants us to consider a radical alternative. Perhaps we should not merely accept but actually admire the conflict. Suffering isn't always the mark of a life going badly. If the well-lived life involves quite a lot of distress, maybe we need to get brave and strong to live it?

The continuous development of art is bound up with the *Apollonian* and *Dionysian* duality – just as procreation depends on the duality of the sexes, involving perpetual strife with only periodically intervening reconciliations.

The terms Dionysian and Apollonian are borrowed from the Greeks, who disclosed the mysteries of their view of art not in concepts but in the intensely clear figures of their gods.

Through Apollo and Dionysus – the two art deities of the Greeks – we come to recognize that in the Greek world there existed a tremendous opposition, in origin and aims, between the Apollonian art of sculpture and the non-imagistic, Dionysian art of music.

These two different tendencies run parallel to one another, for the most part openly at variance; and they continually incite each other to new and more powerful births, which perpetuate the antagonism; till by a miracle of the Greek will they appear coupled with one another, until they create a form of art that is equally Dionysian *and* Apollonian – tragic drama.

In order to grasp these two tendencies, first think of them as the separate worlds of dreams and drunkenness. These psychological phenomena present a contrast similar to that between the Apollonian and the Dionysian.

It was in dreams, says the Roman poet Lucretius, that the glorious divine figures first appeared to the souls of men: in dreams they first beheld the splendid bodies of superhuman beings.

The beautiful illusion of the dream worlds – in the creation of which everyone is truly an artist – is the prerequisite of all plastic art and, as we shall see, an important part of poetry also. In our dreams we delight in the immediate understanding of figures; all forms speak to us; there is nothing unimportant or superfluous. But even when this dream reality is most intense we still have – glimmering through it – the sensation that this is *mere appearance*. At least, this is my experience.

Philosophers have even guessed that the reality in which we live and have our being is also mere appearance and that another, quite different reality, lies beneath it. Schopenhauer actually says it is a sign of philosophical ability to occasionally view men and things as mere phantoms or dream images.

. . .

Perhaps many people will – like myself – recall how amid the dangers and terrors of dreams they have occasionally said to themselves in self-encouragement: 'It is a dream! I will dream on.' . . .

This joyous necessity of the dream experience has been embodied by the Greeks in their Apollo: Apollo, the god of all plastic energies, is at the same time the fortune-telling god. He, who . . . is the 'shining one', the deity of light, is also the ruler over the beautiful illusion of the inner world of fantasy. The higher truth, the perfection of these states in contrast to the incompletely intelligible everyday world, this deep consciousness of nature, healing and helping in sleep and dreams, is – at the same time – the symbolic analogue of the ability to consider the future and of the arts generally, which make life possible and worth living. . . .

We must keep in mind the measured restraint, the freedom from the wilder emotions, the calm of the sculptor-god. His eye must be 'sun-like'. In Apollo there is an unshakeable faith in the *principle of individuation* – each thing is coherent in itself, separate, clearly bounded and distinguished from everything else; everything is what it is, and not confused with anything else. Through the gestures and the eyes of Apollo (as represented in sculpture) all the joy, wisdom and beauty of 'illusion' speak to us.

. . .

But there is a terror and blissful ecstasy that wells from the innermost depths of man, indeed of nature, at the collapse of individuality – and here we steal a first glimpse into the nature of the Dionysian, which is brought home to us most intimately by the analogy of intoxication.

Either under the influence of the narcotic draught – of which all primitive men and peoples speak – or with the potent coming of spring that penetrates all nature with joy, these Dionysian emotions awake, and as they grow in intensity everything private [subjective] vanishes into complete self-forgetfulness. In the German Middle Ages, too, singing and dancing crowds, ever increasing in number, whirled themselves from place to place under this same Dionysian impulse . . .

There are some who from obtuseness or lack of experience turn away from such phenomena as from a disease of the common people with contempt or pity born of their own 'healthy-mindedness'. Of course, such poor wretches have no idea how corpse-like and ghostly their so-called healthy-mindedness looks when the glowing life of the Dionysian revellers roars past them.

Under the charm of the Dionysian not only is the union between man and man reaffirmed, but nature – which has become alien, hostile or subjugated – celebrates once more her reconciliation with her 'lost son': man . . .

In song and dance man expresses himself as a member of a higher community; he has forgotten how to walk and speak and is on the way to flying into the air. His very gestures express enchantment . . .

He becomes a work of art. In these paroxysms of intoxication the artistic power of all nature reveals itself to the highest gratification of the primordial unity.

(*The Birth of Tragedy*, 1872)

Nietzsche is arguing that there is a basic conflict at the root of life. On the one hand we want order, calm, reason and dignity. We want to be in control. We want to sort out our finances, keep the kitchen tidy, be on time, tick off everything on the to-do list, eat moderate and healthy meals (and generally have the 'dream' life). On the other hand, there is a yearning for release, for wild joy and uninhibited desire.

We can find dignity by giving honourable names to both sides of the conflict.

4

THE TROUBLED PATH TO FREEDOM AND MATURITY

....

It would be wonderful if personal development came easily and sweetly – and maybe for some lucky people it does. But often, the path of development – the path to becoming the kind of person you want to be – is rather tortuous and daunting.

Nietzsche tells the story of his own development as a kind of fable. And the lesson is about courage in the face of difficulty. It is normal, he says, to have difficulty growing up. Crucially, freedom involves separation: you have to leave cherished things behind, and leaving them is so hard that you might have to turn against them, for a while – which looks callous and mean, but isn't really.

For parents, this is a hard but ultimately consoling lesson. Your children may go through a period of rejecting you and everything you care for. This is not because they hate you, but because they love you; and to get free – to become independent – they need to break away. For a loving person to break those bonds is so hard that for a while they have to become almost violent and cruel. Nietzsche can't make this easy but he can make it slightly less heartbreaking.

It may be conjectured that the decisive event for a spirit in whom the type of the 'free spirit' is one day to ripen to sweet perfection has been a *great separation*, and that before it, he was probably all the more a bound spirit, and seemed to be chained forever to his corner, to his post. What binds most firmly? Which cords can almost not be torn? With men of a high and select type, it will be their obligations: that awe which befits the young, their diffidence and delicacy before all that is time-honoured and dignified, their gratitude for the ground out of which they grew, for the hand that led them, for the shrine where they learned to worship – their own highest moments will bind them most firmly and oblige them most lastingly. For such bound people the great separation comes suddenly, like the shock of an earthquake: all at once the young soul is devastated, torn loose, torn out – it does not know what is happening. An urge, a pressure governs it, mastering the soul like a command: the will and wish awaken to go away, anywhere, at any cost: a violent, dangerous curiosity for an undiscovered world flames up and flickers in all the senses. 'Better to die than live *here*,' so sounds the imperious and seductive voice. And this 'here', this 'at home' is everything which it had loved until then! A sudden horror and suspicion of that which it loved; a lightning flash of contempt towards that which was its 'obligation'; a rebellious, despotic, volcanically jolting desire to roam abroad, to become alienated, cool, sober, icy: a hatred of love, perhaps a desecratory reaching and glancing *backward*, to where it had until then worshipped and loved; perhaps a blush of shame at its most recent act, and at the same time, jubilation *that* it was done; a drunken, inner, jubilant shudder, which betrays a victory – a victory? over what? over whom? . . .

Such bad and painful things are part of the history of the great separation. It is also a disease that can destroy man, this first outburst of strength and will to self-determination, self-valorization, this will to *free* will: and how much disease is expressed by the wild attempts and peculiarities with which the freed man, the separated man, now tries to prove his rule over things! He wanders about savagely with an unsatisfied lust; his booty must atone for the dangerous tension of his pride; he rips apart what attracts him. With an evil laugh he overturns what he finds concealed, spared until then by some shame; he investigates how these things look if they are overturned. There is some arbitrariness and pleasure in arbitrariness to it, if he then perhaps directs his favour to that which previously stood in disrepute – if he creeps curiously and enticingly around what is most forbidden. Behind his ranging activity (for he is journeying restlessly and aimlessly, as in a desert) stands the question mark of an ever more dangerous curiosity. 'Cannot *all* values be overturned? And is Good perhaps Evil? And God only an invention, a nicety of the devil? Is everything perhaps ultimately false? And if we are deceived, are we not for that very reason also deceivers? *Must* we not be deceivers, too?' Such thoughts lead and mislead him, always further onward, always further away. Loneliness surrounds him, curls round him, ever more threatening, strangling, heart-constricting, that fearful goddess and . . . but who today knows what loneliness is?

It is still a long way from this morbid isolation, from the desert of these experimental years, to that enormous, overflowing certainty and health which cannot do without even illness itself, as an instrument and fish-hook of knowledge; to that *mature* freedom of the spirit which is self-mastery and discipline of the heart, and which permits paths to many opposing ways of thought. It is a long way to the inner spaciousness and cosseting of a superabundance which precludes the danger that the spirit might lose itself on its own paths and fall in love and stay put, intoxicated, in some nook; a long way to that excess of vivid healing, reproducing, reviving powers, the very sign of *great* health, an excess that gives the free spirit the dangerous privilege of being permitted to live *experimentally* and to offer himself to adventure: the privilege of the master free spirit! In between may lie long years of convalescence, years full of multicoloured, painful magical transformations, governed and led by a tough *will to health* which already often dares to dress and disguise itself as health. There is a middle point on the way, which a man having such a fate cannot remember later without being moved: a pale, fine light and sunny happiness are characteristic of it, a feeling of a birdlike freedom, birdlike perspective, birdlike arrogance, some third thing in which curiosity and a tender contempt are united. A 'free spirit' – this cool term is soothing in that state, almost warming. No longer chained down by hatred and love, one lives without Yes, without No, voluntarily near, voluntarily far, most preferably slipping away, avoiding, fluttering on, gone again, flying upward again; one is spoiled, like anyone who has ever seen an enormous multiplicity beneath him – and one becomes the antithesis of those who trouble themselves about things that do not concern them. Indeed, now the free spirit concerns himself only with things (and how many there are!) which no longer *trouble* him.

Another step onward in convalescence. The free spirit again approaches life, slowly, of course, almost recalcitrantly, almost suspiciously. It grows warmer around him again, yellower, as it were; feeling and fellow feeling gain depth; mild breezes of all kinds pass over him. He almost feels as if his eyes were only now open to what is *near*. He is amazed and sits motionless: Where *had he been*, then? These near and nearest things, how they seem to him transformed! What magical fluff they have acquired in the meantime! He glances backward gratefully – grateful to his travels, to his severity and self-alienation, to his far-off glances and bird flights into cold heights. How good that he did not stay 'at home', 'with himself' the whole time, like a dull, pampered loafer! He was *beside* himself: there is no doubt about that. Only now does he see himself – and what surprises he finds there! What untried terrors! What happiness even in weariness, in the old illness, in the convalescent's relapses! How he likes to sit still, suffering, spinning patience, or to lie in the sun! Who understands as he does the happiness of winter, the sun spots on the wall! They are the most grateful animals in the world, the most modest, too, these convalescents and squirrels, turned halfway back to life again – there are those among them who let no day pass without hanging a little song of praise on its trailing hem. And to speak seriously, all pessimism (the inveterate evil of old idealists and liars, as we know) is thoroughly *cured* by falling ill in the way these free spirits do, staying ill for a good while, and then, for even longer, even longer, becoming healthy – I mean 'healthier'. There is wisdom, practical wisdom in it, when over a long period of time even health itself is administered only in small doses.

About that time it may finally happen, among the sudden illuminations of a still turbulent, still changeable state of health, that the free spirit, ever freer, begins to unveil the mystery of that great separation which until then had waited impenetrable, questionable, almost unapproachable in his memory. Perhaps for a long time he hardly dared ask himself: 'Why so apart, so alone? Renouncing everything I admired, even admiration? Why this severity, this suspicion, this hatred of one's own virtues?' But now he dares to ask it loudly, and already hears something like an answer. 'You had to become your own master, and also the master of your own virtues. Previously, your virtues were your masters; but they must be nothing more than your tools, along with your other tools. You had to gain power over your For and Against, and learn how to hang them out or take them in, according to your higher purpose. You had to learn that all estimations have a perspective, to learn the displacement, distortion, apparent teleology of horizons, and whatever else is part of perspective; also the bit of stupidity in regard to opposite values and all the intellectual damage that every For or Against exacts in payment. You had to learn to grasp the *necessary* injustice in every For and Against; to grasp that injustice is inseparable from life, that life itself is *determined* by perspective and its injustice. Above all you had to see clearly wherever injustice is greatest, where life is developed least, most narrowly, meagrely, rudimentarily, and yet cannot help taking *itself* as the purpose and measure of things, and for the sake of its preservation picking at and questioning secretly and pettily and incessantly what is higher, greater and richer. You had to see clearly the problem of *hierarchy*, and how power and justice and breadth of perspective grow upward together. You had to –' Enough, now the free spirit *knows* which 'thou shalt' he has obeyed, and also what he now *can* do, what he only now is *permitted* to do.

(*Human, All Too Human*, 1878)

This is Nietzsche's list of what *he* learned through his own troubled years. The point is not that we should learn the same things; but that we should try to understand what it is that we (and those we are close to) have learned by painful experience.

And finally there is an evocation of the ordinary, simple good things which may once have been ignored or thought not worthy of attention, but which – now – can be appreciated.

Goodwill. Among the small but endlessly abundant and therefore very effective things that science ought to heed more than the great, rare things, is goodwill. I mean those expressions of a friendly disposition in interactions, that smile of the eye, those hand-clasps, that ease which usually envelops nearly all human actions. Every teacher, every official brings this ingredient to what he considers his duty. It is the continual manifestation of our humanity, its rays of light, so to speak, in which everything grows. Especially within the narrowest circle, in the family, life sprouts and blossoms only by this goodwill. Good nature, friendliness and courtesy of the heart are ever-flowing tributaries of the selfless drive and have made much greater contributions to culture than those much more famous expressions of this drive, called pity, charity and self-sacrifice. But we tend to underestimate them, and in fact there really is not much about them that is selfless. The *sum* of these small doses is nevertheless mighty; its cumulative force is among the strongest of forces.

Similarly, there is much more happiness to be found in the world than dim eyes can see, if one calculates correctly and does not forget all those moments of ease which are so plentiful in every day of every human life, even the most oppressed.

(*Human, All Too Human*, 1878)

5

ON CHANGING
ONE'S MIND

....

We change our minds constantly – about great big life-altering issues as well as about the minutiae of daily life. And we have to try to digest the experience. Are we just running away? Is this failure? Have we wasted all those years?

As we have seen, throughout his twenties and early thirties, Nietzsche was very close friends with the great composer Richard Wagner. It was a really exciting relationship. Wagner was very dynamic and ambitious, and Nietzsche loved the music.

But over the years, Nietzsche fell 'out of love', as it were, with Wagner. He came to see his friend as overbearing and a bit hysterical – in fact, even dangerous. This was extremely difficult because Nietzsche had given Wagner extensive praise in print, and had been a very loyal and public supporter for many years, so it was a kind of divorce. Wagner was intensely hurt and angry. But Nietzsche had to explain to himself what it was all about. Had he just wasted ten years of his life in a deep friendship with someone who, on balance, wasn't good for him?

It is one thing to change your mind – that happens all the time, often without us really being aware that is happening – but we also want to learn how to grow and develop through changing our minds.

First, we see Nietzsche at the high-water mark of enthusiasm for Wagner. He wants to tell the whole world what is wonderful about his friend's mind. It is a very philosophical answer to an ordinary question: Why do you like him so much?

Wagner concentrated upon life, past and present, the light of an intelligence strong enough to embrace the most distant regions in its rays. That is why he is a simplifier of the universe; for the simplification of the universe is only possible to him whose eye has been able to master the immensity and wildness of an apparent chaos, and to relate and unite those things which before had lain hopelessly asunder. Wagner did this by discovering a connection between two objects which seemed to exist apart from each other as though in separate spheres – that between music and life, and similarly between music and the drama. Not that he invented or was the first to create this relationship, for they must always have existed and have been noticeable to all; but, as is usually the case with a great problem, it is like a precious stone which thousands stumble over before one finally picks it up. Wagner asked himself the meaning of the fact that an art such as music should have become so very important a feature of the lives of modern men. It is not necessary to think meanly of life in order to suspect a riddle behind this question. On the contrary, when all the great forces of existence are duly considered, and struggling life is regarded as striving mightily after conscious freedom and independence of thought, only then does music seem to be a riddle in this world. Should one not answer: Music could not have been born in our time? What then does its presence amongst us signify? An accident? A single great artist might certainly be an accident, but the appearance of a whole group of them, such as the history of modern music has to show, a group only once before equalled on earth, that is to say in the time of the Greeks – a circumstance of this sort leads one to think that perhaps necessity rather than accident is at the root of the whole phenomenon. The meaning of this necessity is the riddle which Wagner answers.

He was the first to recognize an evil which is as widespread as civilization itself among men; language is everywhere diseased, and the burden of this terrible disease weighs heavily upon the whole of man's development. Inasmuch as language has retreated ever more and more from its true province – the expression of strong feelings, which it was once able to convey in all their simplicity – and has always had to strain after the practically impossible achievement of communicating the reverse of feeling, that is to say thought, its strength has become so exhausted by this excessive extension of its duties during the comparatively short period of modern civilization, that it is no longer able to perform even that function which alone justifies its existence, to wit, the assisting of those who suffer, in communicating with each other concerning the sorrows of existence. Man can no longer make his misery known unto others by means of language; hence he cannot really express himself any longer. And under these conditions, which are only vaguely felt at present, language has gradually become a force in itself which with spectral arms coerces and drives humanity where it least wants to go. As soon as they would fain understand one another and unite for a common cause, the craziness of general concepts, and even of the ring of modern words, lays hold of them. The result of this inability to communicate with one another is that every product of their cooperative action bears the stamp of discord, not only because it fails to meet their real needs, but because of the very emptiness of those all-powerful words and notions already mentioned. To the misery already at hand, man thus adds the curse of convention – that is to say, the agreement between words and actions without an agreement between the feelings. Just as, during the decline of every art, a point is reached when the morbid accumulation of its means and forms attains to such tyrannical proportions that it oppresses the tender souls of artists and converts these into slaves, so now, in the period of the decline of language, men have become the slaves of words. Under this yoke no one is able to show himself as he is, or to express himself artlessly, while only few are able to preserve their individuality in their fight against a culture which thinks to manifest its success, not by the fact that it approaches definite sensations and desires with the view of educating them, but by the fact that it involves the individual in the snare of 'definite notions', and teaches him to think correctly: as if there were any value in making a correctly thinking and reasoning being out of man, before one has succeeded in making him a creature that feels correctly. If now the strains of our German masters' music burst upon a mass of mankind sick to this extent, what is really the meaning of these strains? Only correct feeling, the enemy of all convention, of all artificial estrangement and misunderstandings between man and man: this music signifies a return to nature, and at the same time a purification and remodelling of it; for the need of such a return

took shape in the souls of the most loving of men,
and, through their art, nature transformed into love
makes its voice heard.

(*Richard Wagner in Bayreuth*, 1876)

This is abstract, but it hints at passion: my friend is
fascinating, he does interesting things. My friend and
I are free of convention; *we* can really communicate
with each other because *we* have mutual agreement as
to feelings.

After a break-up, the important thing to understand
as accurately as possible is why that person was bad for
you. Nietzsche tends to sounds as if he is preaching
to the whole world; but the person who most needs
to learn the lesson of insight is, of course, himself. In
doing so, he goes to the heart of what attracted him
to his friend in the first place – his power as a musi-
cian (but in more normal scenarios it might be witty
conversation, fashion sense, inspiring sexual persona
or confidence around money). Maturing in one's relation to that attractive quality can be what is involved
in outgrowing someone. Nietzsche came to love the
music of Bizet, especially *Carmen*. And this new love
let him see what wasn't working in the old relationship.

You begin to see how much Bizet's music improves
me? . . . The return to nature, health, cheerfulness,
virtue. And yet I was one of the most corrupted

Wagnerians – I was capable of taking Wagner seriously. Ah! this old magician, how much he imposed on us! The first thing his art offers us is a magnifying glass: one looks through it, one does not trust one's own eyes – everything looks big, *even Wagner.*
. . .

One pays heavily for being one of Wagner's disciples – that is, for being his friend. What does it do to the spirit? *Does Wagner liberate the spirit?* He is distinguished by every ambiguity, every double sense, everything quite generally that persuades those who are uncertain without making them aware *of what* they have been persuaded. Thus Wagner is a seducer on a large scale. There is nothing weary, nothing decrepit, nothing fatal and hostile to life in matters of the spirit that his art does not secretly safeguard; it is the blackest obscurantism that he conceals in the ideal's shafts of light. He flatters every nihilistic instinct and disguises it in music; he flatters . . . every religious expression of decadence. Open your ears: everything that ever grew in the soil of *impoverished* life, all the counterfeiting of transcendence and beyond, has found its most sublime advocate in Wagner's art – *not* by means of formulas: Wagner is too shrewd for formulas – but by means of a persuasion of sensuousness which in turn makes the spirit weary and worn-out.

(*The Case of Wagner,* 1888)

He finally nails the problem:

> For a long time Wagner's ship gaily followed a utopian, optimistic course. No doubt this was where Wagner sought his highest goal: free love, a socialist utopia, where all turns out well. What happened? A misfortune. His ship struck a reef; Wagner was stuck. The reef was Schopenhauer's pessimistic philosophy [by which Wagner was terribly impressed]; Wagner was stranded; Wagner was stranded on someone else's *contrary* world view. Wagner was ashamed. His instinctive optimism was one for which Schopenhauer has coined an evil name: *infamous* optimism. He was even more ashamed. He reflected for a long time, his situation seemed desperate. – Finally a way out dawned on him: the reef on which he was shipwrecked – what if he interpreted it as the *goal*, as the secret intent, as the true significance of his voyage? To be shipwrecked *here*, that was the goal. Everything must go wrong, everything perishes, the new world must be as bad as the old.
>
> (*The Case of Wagner*, 1888)

So he diagnoses his friend's problem: he is an instinctive optimist who thinks, really, that optimism isn't enough. So he then turns round and attacks his own optimism – and preaches this to the world as the deepest and cleverest possible view of life. And because a lot of people are confused in their own minds between the instincts of cheerfulness and despair, this ruse is highly seductive.

In other words, Nietzsche can forgive himself for being taken in. Instead of simply saying: 'What an idiot I was ever to get mixed up with that person,' he now understands what went wrong; he can learn from this and avoid repeating the mistake.

6

THE MERITS OF
SHOCK THERAPY

....

The atmosphere of our times – the collective values of decent people – enters so deeply into our assumptions that we almost stop noticing. Nietzsche was keen on shocking his readers, firing off a string of incredibly hostile insights against the very things which we assume we must revere: democracy, the importance of pity and compassion, the value of community, the pursuit of the common good. The use of these cruel assertions is to let us try out, even if only for a few minutes, what it would be like not to share the basic assumptions of our times.

Talking of people as 'herds' as Nietzsche does in the following extract can come across as mean. But it is the risk he takes in order to jolt us into recognition of some unpalatable but serious thoughts. Maybe at times we are a bit too preoccupied with fitting in; maybe we have in some ways become timid, in our fear of confrontation. Obviously, this does not apply to everyone: what useful lesson could? The underlying question is this: does fear rule your life too much?

Are your ideas about life mainly ways of protecting yourself?

Inasmuch as ever since there have been human beings there have also been human herds (family groups, communities, tribes, nations, states, churches), and always very many who obey compared with the very small number of those who command – considering, that is to say, that hitherto nothing has been practised and cultivated among men better or longer than obedience, it is fair to suppose that as a rule a need for it is by now innate as a kind of *formal conscience* which commands: 'Thou shalt unconditionally do this, unconditionally not do that', in short 'Thou shalt'. This need seeks to be satisfied and to fill out its form with a content; in doing so it grasps about wildly, according to the degree of its strength, impatience and tension, with little discrimination, as a crude appetite, and accepts whatever any commander – parent, teacher, law, class prejudice, public opinion – shouts in its ears. The strange narrowness of human evolution, its hesitations, its delays, its frequent retrogressions and rotations, are due to the fact that the herd instinct of obedience has been inherited best and at the expense of the art of commanding. If we think of this instinct taken to its ultimate extravagance there would be no commanders or independent men at all; or, if they existed, they would suffer from a bad conscience and

in order to be able to command would have to practise a deceit upon themselves: the deceit, that is,
that they too were only obeying. This state of things
actually exists in Europe today: I call it the moral
hypocrisy of the commanders. They know no way of
defending themselves against their bad conscience
other than to pose as executors of more ancient or
higher commands (commands of ancestors, of the
constitution, of justice, of the law or even of God), or
even to borrow herd maxims from the herd's way of
thinking and appear as 'the first servant of the people'
for example, or as 'instruments of the common good'.
On the other hand, the herd-man in Europe today
makes himself out to be the only permissible kind
of man and glorifies the qualities through which he
is tame, peaceable and useful to the herd as the
real human virtues: namely public spirit, benevo-
lence, consideration, industriousness, moderation,
modesty, forbearance, pity.

(Beyond Good and Evil, 1886)

It is hardly a bad list. His point is that it misses out too
much. He is probing the trade-off we make between
the desire for domestic peace and quiet and the will to
argue, struggle, demand, order, fight.

So long as the utility which dominates moral value
judgements is solely that which is useful to the herd,

so long as the object is solely the preservation of the community and the immoral is sought precisely and exclusively in that which seems to imperil the existence of the community: so long as that is the case there can be no 'morality of love of one's neighbour'. Supposing that even there a constant little exercise of consideration, pity, fairness, mildness, mutual aid was practised, supposing that even at that stage of society all those drives are active which are later honourably designated 'virtues' and are finally practically equated with the concept 'morality': in that era they do not yet by any means belong to the domain of moral valuations – they are still *extra-moral*. An act of pity, for example, was during the finest age of Rome considered neither good nor bad, neither moral nor immoral; and even if it was commended, this commendation was entirely compatible with a kind of involuntary disdain, as soon, that is, as it was set beside any action which served the welfare of the whole, of the *res publica*. Ultimately 'love of one's neighbour' is always something secondary, in part conventional and arbitrarily illusory, when compared with *fear of one's neighbour*. Once the structure of society seems to have been in general fixed and made safe from external dangers, it is this fear of one's neighbour which again creates new perspectives of moral valuation. There are certain strong and dangerous drives, such as enterprise, foolhardiness, revengefulness, craft, rapacity, ambition, which hitherto had not only to be honoured from the point of view of their social utility – under different names, naturally, from those chosen here – but also mightily developed and cultivated (because they were constantly needed to protect the community as a whole against the enemies of the community as a whole); these drives are now felt to be doubly dangerous – now that the diversionary outlets for them are lacking – and are gradually branded as immoral and given over to calumny. The antithetical drives and inclinations now come into moral honour; step by step the herd instinct draws its conclusions. How much or how little that is dangerous to the community, dangerous to equality, resides in an opinion, in a condition or emotion, in a will, in a talent, that is now the moral perspective: here again fear is the mother of morality. When the highest and strongest drives, breaking passionately out, carry the individual far above and beyond the average and lowlands of the herd conscience, the self-confidence of the community goes to pieces, its faith in itself, its spine as it were, is broken: consequently it is precisely these drives which are most branded and calumniated. Lofty spiritual independence, the will to stand alone, great intelligence even, are felt to be dangerous; everything that raises the individual above the herd and makes his neighbour quail is henceforth called *evil*; the fair, modest, obedient, self-effacing disposition, the *mean and average* in desires, acquires moral names and honours. Eventually, under very peaceful conditions, there is less and less occasion or need to educate one's feelings in severity and sternness; and now every kind of severity, even severity in justice, begins to trouble the conscience; a stern and lofty nobility and self-responsibility is received almost as an offence and awakens mistrust; 'the lamb', even more 'the sheep', is held in higher and higher respect. There comes a point of morbid mellowing and over-tenderness in the history of society at which it takes the side even of him who harms it, the *criminal*, and does so honestly and wholeheartedly. Punishment: that seems to it somehow unfair – certainly the idea of 'being punished' and 'having to punish' is unpleasant to it, makes it afraid. 'Is it not enough to render him *harmless*? Why punish him as well? To administer punishment is itself dreadful!' With this question herd morality, the morality of timidity, draws its ultimate conclusion. Supposing all danger, the cause of fear, could be abolished, this morality would therewith also be abolished: it would no longer be necessary, it would no longer *regard itself* as necessary! – He who examines the conscience of the present-day European will have to extract from a thousand moral recesses and hiding places always the same imperative, the imperative of herd timidity: 'We wish for the day that there will *no longer be anything to fear!*' One day everywhere in Europe the way to that day is now called 'progress'. . .

We know well enough how offensive it sounds when someone says plainly and without metaphor that man is an animal; but it will be reckoned almost a *crime* in us that precisely in regard to men of 'modern ideas' we constantly employ the terms 'herd', 'herd instinct', and the like. But what of that! We can do no other: for it is precisely here that our new insight lies. We have found that in all principal moral judgements Europe has become unanimous, including the lands where Europe's influence predominates: one manifestly *knows* in Europe what Socrates thought he did not know, and what that celebrated old serpent once promised to teach – one 'knows' today what is good and evil. Now it is bound to make a harsh sound and one not easy for ears to hear when we insist again and again: that which here believes it knows, that which here glorifies itself with its praising and blaming and calls itself good, is the instinct of the herd-animal man: the instinct which has broken through and come to predominate and prevail over the other instincts and is coming to do so more and more in proportion to the increasing physiological approximation and assimilation of which it is the symptom. *Morality is in Europe today herd-animal morality* – that is to say, as we understand the thing, only one kind of human morality beside which, before which, after which many other, above all *higher*, moralities are possible or ought to be possible. But against such a 'possibility', against such an 'ought', this morality defends itself with all its might: it says, obstinately and stubbornly: 'I am morality itself, and nothing is morality besides me!' – Indeed, with the aid of a religion which has gratified and flattered the sublimest herd-animal desires, it has got to the point where we discover even in political and social institutions an increasingly evident expression of this morality: the *democratic* movement inherits the Christian. But that the tempo of this movement is much too slow and somnolent for the more impatient, for the sick and suffering of the said instinct, is attested by the ever more frantic baying, the ever more undisguised fang-baring of the anarchist dogs which now rove the streets of European culture: apparently the reverse of the placidly industrious democrats and revolutionary ideologists, and even more so of the stupid philosophasters and brotherhood fanatics who call themselves socialists and want a 'free society'. They are in fact at one with them all in their total and instinctive hostility towards every form of society other than that of the *autonomous* herd (to the point of repudiating even the concepts 'master' and 'servant' – *ni dieu ni maître* says a socialist formula –); at one in their tenacious opposition to every special claim, every special right and privilege (that is to say, in the last resort to *every* right: for when everyone is equal no one will need any 'rights'); at one in their mistrust of punitive justice (as if it were an assault on the weaker, an injustice against the necessary conse-quence of all previous society); but equally at one in the religion of pity, in sympathy with whatever feels, lives, suffers (down as far as the animals, up as far, as 'God' the extravagance of 'pity for God' belongs in a democratic era); at one, one and all, in the cry and impatience of pity, in mortal hatred for suffering in general, in their almost feminine incapacity to remain spectators of suffering, to *let* suffer; at one in their involuntary gloom and sensitivity, under whose spell Europe seems threatened with a new Buddhism; at one in their faith in the morality of *mutual* pity, as if it were morality in itself and the pinnacle, the *attained* pinnacle of man, the sole hope of the future, the consolation of the present and the great redemption from all the guilt of the past – at one, one and all, in their faith in the community as the *saviour*, that is to say in the herd, in 'themselves' . . .

(*Beyond Good and Evil*, 1886)

67

Nietzsche pushed the point even further in a later book called *The Gay Science*, 1882. (The title signifies 'joyful knowledge' – the knowledge that helps us to be cheerful and to remain in good spirits, in the face of the troubles life throws at us.)

> I welcome all signs that a more virile, warlike age is about to begin, which will restore honour to courage above all. For this age shall prepare the way for one yet higher, and it shall gather the strength that this higher age will require some day – the age that will carry heroism into the search for knowledge and that will wage wars for the sake of ideas and their consequences.
>
> (*The Gay Science*, 1882)

The first instinct is, perhaps, to recoil from the very mention of war. But Nietzsche is not submitting an eccentric report to the Ministry of Defence or the Pentagon. Rather, to get beauty and wisdom to prevail in the world is a task *like* a war, requiring the same level of devotion and the same degree of mobilization of resources and effort.

> To this end we now need many preparatory courageous human beings who cannot very well leap out of nothing, any more than out of the sand and slime of present-day civilization and metropolitanism – human

beings who know how to be silent, lonely, resolute, and content and constant in invisible activities; human beings who are bent on seeking in all things for what in them must be overcome; human beings distinguished as much by cheerfulness, patience, unpretentiousness, and contempt for all great vanities as by magnanimity in victory and forbearance regarding the small vanities of the vanquished; human beings whose judgement concerning all victors and the share of chance in every victory and fame is sharp and free; human beings with their own festivals, their own working days, and their own periods of mourning, accustomed to command with assurance but instantly ready to obey when that is called for – equally proud, equally serving their own cause in both cases; more endangered human beings, more fruitful human beings, happier beings! For believe me: the secret for harvesting from existence the greatest fruitfulness and the greatest enjoyment is – to live dangerously. Build your cities on the slopes of Vesuvius! Send your ships into uncharted seas! Live at war with your peers and yourselves!

(*The Gay Science*, 1882)

Of course, brave and experimental thinking does not help you fit in. Nietzsche tries to imagine the kind of friends he needs:

What I always needed most to cure and restore myself, however, was the belief that I was *not* the only one to be thus, to *see* thus – I needed the enchanting intuition of kinship and equality in the eye and in desire, repose in a trusted friendship; I needed a shared blindness, with no suspicion or question marks, a pleasure in foregrounds, surfaces, what is near, what is nearest, in everything that has colour, skin, appearance.

. . .

Thus I invented, when I needed them, the 'free spirits' too, to whom this heavy-hearted- stout-hearted book with the title 'Human, All Too Human' is dedicated. There are no such 'free spirits', were none – but, as I said, I needed their company at the time, to be of good cheer in the midst of bad things (illness, isolation, foreignness, sloth, inactivity); as brave fellows and spectres to chat and laugh with, when one feels like chatting and laughing, and whom one sends to hell when they get boring – as reparation for lacking friends. That there *could* some day be such free spirits, that our Europe will have such lively, daring fellows among its sons of tomorrow and the day after tomorrow, real and palpable and not merely, as in my case, phantoms and a hermit's shadow play: I am the last person to want to doubt that. I already see them *coming*, slowly, slowly; and perhaps I am doing something to hasten their coming when I describe before the fact the fateful conditions that I *see* giving rise to them, the paths on which I *see* them coming?

(Human, All Too Human, 1878)

7

BE A NOBLE
NOT A SLAVE

....

Sometimes we need to recognize – and with any luck overcome – entrenched biases in our own characters. We might need a strong dose of something we are missing. It isn't the whole truth, but it is a part of the truth we need to attend to, because it is the bit we lack.

Nietzsche thought that we are often (without realizing it) passive and reactive. We don't think and feel and act for ourselves. We are not 'noble' enough. In fact we are frightened. And in our fear we tell ourselves falsely consoling stories: I didn't really want that promotion; I don't really want to make a lot of money (and inequality is wrong anyway). He wants to waken a kind of inner aristocrat who doesn't much care what others think and just gets on with being who they really are.

At times Nietzsche sounds incredibly snobbish. It makes more sense – and is more useful to us – when we keep in mind that Nietzsche was not himself especially like the nobles he so admires. That is a compensating, corrective vision which he makes for himself. Rather than reading this as a discussion of two different kinds of people, it is helpful to regard it as a discussion of contending aspects of one person. It enables us to see more clearly certain aspects – noble and base – of our own character.

The idea that power is bad, that the strong and dominating are the enemy, is one that occurs very naturally to almost everyone.

> The slave revolt in morality begins when *ressentiment* [French for 'resentment'] itself becomes creative and gives birth to values: the *ressentiment* of natures that are denied the true reaction, that of deeds, and compensate themselves with an imaginary revenge. While every noble morality develops from a triumphant affirmation of itself, slave morality from the outset says No to what is 'outside', what is 'different', what is 'not itself'; and *this* No is its creative deed. This inversion of the value-positing eye – this *need* to direct one's view outward instead of back to oneself – is of the essence of *ressentiment*; in order to exist, slave morality always first needs a hostile external world; it needs, physiologically speaking, external stimuli in order to act at all – its action is fundamentally reaction.
>
> One should not overlook the almost benevolent nuances that the Greek nobility, for example, bestows on all the words it employs to distinguish the lower orders from itself; how they are continuously mingled and sweetened with a kind of pity, consideration and

forbearance, so that finally almost all the words referring to the common man have remained as expressions signifying 'unhappy', 'pitiable' – and how on the other hand 'bad', 'low', 'unhappy' have never ceased to sound to the Greek ear as one note with a tone-colour in which 'unhappy' preponderates: this as an inheritance from the ancient nobler aristocratic mode of evaluation, which does not belie itself even in its contempt. The 'well-born' *felt* themselves to be the 'happy'; they did not have to establish their happiness artificially by examining their enemies, or to persuade themselves, *deceive* themselves, that they were happy (as all men of *ressentiment* are in the habit of doing); and they likewise knew, as rounded men replete with energy and therefore *necessarily* active, that happiness should not be sundered from action – being active was with them necessarily a part of happiness – all very much the opposite of 'happiness' at the level of the impotent, the oppressed, and those in whom poisonous and inimical feelings are festering.

While the noble man lives in trust and openness with himself, the man of *ressentiment* is neither upright nor naive nor honest and straightforward with himself. His soul *squints;* his spirit loves hiding places, secret paths and back doors, everything covert entices him as *his* world, *his* security, *his* refreshment; he understands how to keep silent, how not to forget, how to wait, how to be provisionally self-deprecating and humble. A race of such men of *ressentiment* is bound to become eventually *cleverer* than any noble race; it will also honour cleverness to a far greater degree: namely, as a condition of existence of the first importance; while with nobler men cleverness can easily acquire a subtle flavour of luxury and subtlety – for here it is far less essential than the perfect functioning of the regulating *unconscious* instincts or even a certain imprudence, perhaps a bold recklessness whether in the face of danger or of the enemy, or enthusiastic impulsiveness in anger, love, reverence, gratitude and revenge by which noble souls have at all times recognized one another. *Ressentiment* itself, if it should appear in the noble man, consummates and exhausts itself in an immediate reaction, and therefore does not *poison*: on the other hand, it fails to appear at all on countless occasions on which it inevitably appears in the weak and impotent.

To be incapable of taking one's enemies, one's accidents, even one's misdeeds seriously for very long – that is the sign of strong, full natures in whom there is an excess of the power to form, to mould, to recuperate and to forget. Such a man shakes off with a single *shrug* many vermin that eat deep into others; here alone genuine 'love of one's enemies' is possible – supposing it to be possible at all on earth. How much reverence has a noble man for his enemies! – and such reverence is a bridge to love. – For he desires his enemy for himself, as his mark of distinction; he can endure no other enemy than one in whom there is nothing to despise and *very much* to honour! In contrast to this, picture 'the enemy' as the man of *ressentiment* conceives him – and here precisely is his deed, his creation: he has conceived 'the evil enemy', *'the Evil One'*, and this in fact is his basic concept, from which he then evolves, as an afterthought and pendant, a 'good one' – himself!

. . .

This, then, is quite the contrary of what the noble man does, who conceives the basic concept 'good' in advance and spontaneously out of himself and only then creates for himself an idea of 'bad'! This 'bad' of noble origin and that 'evil' out of the cauldron of unsatisfied hatred – the former an after-production, a side issue, a contrasting shade, the latter on the contrary the original thing, the beginning, the distinctive *deed* in the conception of a slave morality – how different these words 'bad' and 'evil' are, although they are both apparently the opposite of the same concept 'good'. But it is *not* the same concept 'good': one should ask rather precisely *who* is 'evil' in the sense of the morality of *ressentiment*. The answer, in all strictness, is: *precisely* the good man' of the other morality, precisely the noble, powerful man.

. . .

That lambs dislike great birds of prey does not seem strange: only it gives no grounds for reproaching these birds of prey for bearing off little lambs. And if the lambs say among themselves: 'These birds of prey are evil; and whoever is least like a bird of prey, but rather its opposite, a lamb – would he not be good?' there is no reason to find fault with this institution of an ideal, except perhaps that the birds of prey might view it a little ironically and say: '*We* don't dislike them at all, these good little lambs; we even love them: nothing is more tasty than a tender lamb.'

To demand of strength that it should *not* express itself as strength, that it should *not* be a desire to overcome, a desire to throw down, a desire to become master, a thirst for enemies and resistances and triumphs, is just as absurd as to demand of weakness that it should express itself as strength. A quantum of force is equivalent to a quantum of drive, will, effect – more, it is nothing other than precisely this very driving, willing, effecting, and only owing to the seduction of language (and of the fundamental errors of reason that petrified in it) which conceives and misconceives all effects as conditioned by something that causes effects, by a subject', can it appear otherwise. For just as the popular mind separates the lightning from its flash and takes the latter for an *action*, for the operation of a subject called lightning, so popular morality also separates strength from expressions of strength, as if there were a neutral substratum behind the strong man, which was *free* to express strength or not to do so. But there is no such substratum; there is no 'being' behind doing, effecting, becoming; 'the doer' is merely a fiction added to the deed – the deed is everything. The popular mind in fact doubles the deed; when it sees the lightning flash, it is the deed of a deed: it posits the same event first as cause and then a second time as its effect. Scientists do no better when they say 'force moves', 'force causes', and the like – all its coolness, its freedom from emotion notwithstanding, our entire science still lies under the misleading influence of language and has not disposed of that little changeling, the 'subject' (the atom, for example, is such a changeling, as is the Kantian 'thing-in-itself'); no wonder if the submerged, darkly glowering emotions of vengeful-ness and hatred exploit this belief for their own ends and in fact maintain no belief more ardently than the belief that *the strong man is free* to be weak and the bird of prey to be a lamb – for thus they gain the right to make the bird of prey *accountable* for being a bird of prey.

The oppressed, downtrodden, outraged exhort one another with the vengeful cunning of impotence: 'Let us be different from the evil, namely good! And he is good who does not outrage, who harms nobody, who does not attack, who does not requite, who leaves revenge to God, who keeps himself hidden as we do, who avoids evil and desires little from life, like us, the patient, humble, and just' . . .

(*On the Genealogy of Morality*, 1887)

Nietzsche now imagines a kind of underground factory in which actual weakness is converted into fake morality; things that are merely matters of powerlessness (like a lamb being unable to take revenge on an eagle) are fabricated into moral attitudes. This is really a story about how – in our own moments of weakness – we hide what is really going on. Instead of strengthening ourselves for competition, we blame others, and then pat ourselves on the back for not being like those dreadful people.

Weakness is being lied into something *meritorious*, no doubt of it . . . and impotence which does not requite into 'goodness of heart'; anxious lowliness into 'humility'; subjection to those one hates into 'obedience' (that is, to one of whom they say he commands this subjection – they call him God). The inoffensiveness of the weak man, even the cowardice of which he has so much, his lingering at the door, his being ineluctably compelled to wait, here acquire flattering names, such as 'patience', and are even called virtue itself; his inability for revenge is called unwillingness to revenge, perhaps even forgiveness . . .

(On the Genealogy of Morality, 1887)

There are plenty of people who are too arrogant already. But there are lots of decent people who are not arrogant enough. Don't complain that the Cabinet is stuffed with idiots, or that bankers are crooks, but instead compete, do it better.

8

DON'T PULL
YOUR PUNCHES

....

There are always people we disagree with, people we dislike, people who annoy or irritate us. It's tempting simply to ignore them – why waste our attention? Even more tempting, perhaps, is the response of caricature: that person is demonized, everything they do is idiotic. Nietzsche (who was unusually adroit in making enemies) pursues another path. He asks himself quite seriously: what really is going wrong here? What exactly do I find troubling about this person? In other words the goal is understanding. The basic point is that when you have a strong experience – negative, as here, or indeed positive – you do not automatically have insight into what it means. You learn from your experience not simply by having it, but by analysing it.

This strategy is exemplified in an essay Nietzsche devoted to the now little-known, but in those days extremely successful, German author David Strauss. He studies Strauss as a representative man: as the clearest instance of a kind of person that really bothers him. He thinks of this kind of person as 'the scientific man' or 'the educated philistine'. (By way of clarification, Nietzsche uses 'science' in a broad sense to encompass not only the natural sciences but also the human sciences, or humanities, which is why he often refers to scholars and scientists interchangeably.)

We all know that our age is typified by its pursuit of science; we know it because it is part of our life: and that precisely is the reason almost no one asks himself what the consequences of such an involvement with the sciences could be for culture . . .

For the nature of scientific man . . . contains a real paradox: he behaves like the proudest well-off idler, as though existence were not a dreadful and questionable thing but a firm possession guaranteed to last for ever. He seems to be permitted to squander his life on questions whose answers could at bottom be of consequence only to someone assured of eternity . . .

The heir of but a few hours, he is ringed around with frightful abysses, and every step he takes ought to make him ask: Where from? Where to? To what end? But his soul is warmed with the task of counting the stamens of a flower or breaking up the stones of the pathway, and all the interest, joy, strength and desire he possesses is absorbed in this work. Now this paradox – this scientific man – has in recent years got into a frantic hurry, as though science were a factory and every minute's slacking incurred punishment. He looks neither to left nor right and goes through all the business of life semi-conscious or with the repellent craving for entertainment characteristic of the exhausted worker.

And this is his attitude towards culture too. He behaves as though life were to him not only idleness, but idleness without dignity. Our scholars are hardly to be distinguished from farmers who want to increase the tiny property they have inherited and are assiduously employed all day and far into the night in tilling the field, leading the plough and encouraging the oxen. Now, Pascal believes quite generally that men pursue their business and their sciences so eagerly only so as to elude the most important questions which would press upon them in a state of solitude or if they were truly idle, that is to say precisely those questions as to: Where to? Where from? And: Why? Amazingly, the most obvious question fails to occur to our scholars: What is their work, their hurry, their painful frenzy supposed to be for? To earn bread or acquire positions of honour, perhaps? Not at all. Yet you exert yourselves like those in need of food, indeed you tear if from the table of science as greedily and as utterly unselectively as though you were on the point of starvation. But if you, as men of science, treat science in the way a worker treats the tasks that are to furnish his means of life, what will become of a culture condemned to await the hour of its birth and redemption in the midst of such agitation and breathless confusion? No one has time for it – and yet, what is science for *at all*, if it has no time for culture? At least reply to this question: what is the 'Where from?' the 'Where to?' and the 'To what end?' of science – if it isn't to lead us to culture? To lead us to barbarism, perhaps?

One is reminded of the social world of the learned classes where when the shop-talk is exhausted there is evidence only of weariness, of a desire for diversion at any price, of a tattered memory and incoherent personal experience. When we hear Strauss speak of the problems of life – whether it be the problem of marriage or of war or of capital punishment – we are appalled at his lack of real experience, of any native insight into the nature of man; all his judgements are so uniformly bookish, indeed at bottom merely of the sort found in the newspapers; literary reminiscences take the place of genuine ideas and insights.

How exactly this corresponds to the spirit which informs the noisily advertised high seats of learning in the cities of Germany! How congenial this spirit must find the spirit of Strauss, for it is in precisely those places that culture is most completely lacking, it is precisely there that the germination of a new culture is totally thwarted; noisy preparation for the sciences there pursued goes with a herd-like stampede for the discipline most in favour at the cost of deserting those of the most consequence.

. . . Viewed externally, these places display all the pomp of culture; with their imposing apparatus they resemble an arsenal choked with cannon and other weapons of war; we behold such preparations and industrious activity as though heaven itself were to be stormed and truth fetched up out of the deepest well, and yet in warfare it is often the biggest pieces of apparatus that are worst deployed. Genuine culture likewise avoids these places as it conducts its campaigns, feeling instinctively that it has nothing to hope for and much to fear in them. For the only form of culture with which the inflamed eye and the blunted brain of the learned working [i.e. scientific/ scholarly] class want to occupy themselves with is precisely that *philistine culture* whose gospel has been proclaimed by Strauss.

. . .

The word 'philistine' . . . signifies, in its wider . . . sense, the antithesis of a son of the muses, of the artists of the person of genuine culture. The cultural philistine however . . . distinguishes himself from the general idea of the species 'philistine' through a superstition: he fancies himself a son of the muses, and a person of culture; a . . . delusion which reveals that he does not even know what a philistine is. With this lack of all self-knowledge he feels firmly

> convinced that his 'culture' is the complete expres-
> sion of true ... culture; and since he everywhere
> discovers cultivated people of his own kind, and
> finds all public institutions, schools and cultural and
> artistic bodies organized in accordance with his kind
> of cultivation and in the service of his requirements,
> he also bears with him everywhere the trium-
> phant feeling of being the worthy representative of
> contemporary ... culture and frames his demands
> and pretensions accordingly.
>
> (*David Strauss, the Confessor and the Writer*, 1873)

The value of the punch does not lie in how hard it is, but the degree to which it is on target. Rather than just being angry and disgusted with Strauss – and even more with those who laud him – Nietzsche takes this as an occasion to try to understand what is going wrong here; what really is it about Strauss that he dislikes so much, and hence feels so threatened by that he must strike out at it? The point isn't so much to try to hurt Strauss, but to know himself.

CONCLUSION:
ON KEEPING A NOTEBOOK

....

The utility of musing, pondering and speculating is not always obvious, although it is generally something we enjoy doing. A lot of practical concerns are focused on what is directly ahead. So big, swirling thoughts seem almost like the opposite of what is useful. But sometimes there is a pay-off. It depends upon how we muse. One key idea is perspective: we can reframe our immediate concerns in the light of a bigger picture. But immediate concerns do not themselves provide that picture.

We can see how this works by looking at one of the ideas Nietzsche eventually became famous for, provocative assertion: 'God is dead.'

Have you not heard of that madman who lit a lantern in the bright morning hours, ran to the marketplace and cried incessantly: 'I am looking for God! I am looking for God!' – Because many of those who did not believe in God were standing together there he excited considerable laughter. 'Have you lost him then?' said one. 'Did he lose his way like a child?' said another. 'Or is he hiding? Is he afraid of us? Has he gone on a voyage? Or emigrated?' – Thus they shouted and laughed. The madman sprang into their midst and pierced them with his glances. 'I shall tell you. *We have killed him* – you and I. We are all his murderers. But how have we done this? How were we able to drink up the sea? Who gave us the sponge to wipe away the entire horizon? What did we do when we unchained this earth from its sun? Whither is it moving now? Whither are we moving now? Away from all suns? Are we not perpetually falling? Backwards, sidewards, forwards, in all directions? Is there any up or down left? Are we not straying as through an infinite nothing? Do we not feel the breath of empty space? Has it not become colder? Is not getting darker and darker all the time? Must not lanterns be lit in the morning? Do we not hear anything yet but the noise of the gravediggers who are burying God? Do we not smell anything yet of God's decomposition? – Gods too decompose. God is dead. God remains dead. And we have killed him. How shall we, the murderers of all murderers, console ourselves? That which was holiest and mightiest of all that the world has yet possessed has bled to death under our knives – who will wipe this blood off us? With what water could we purify ourselves? What festivals of atonement, what sacred

> games shall we need to invent? Is not the greatness
> of this deed too great for us? Must not we ourselves
> become gods simply to seem worthy of it?'
>
> (*The Gay Science*, 1882)

Surprisingly, Nietzsche is not really describing a conflict between Christians and atheists. His target here is what he thinks of as the light-minded atheist. The end of profound religious faith strikes Nietzsche as almost a crime (even though he is a non-believer). He is deeply impressed by the majestic imaginative power of the idea of God; he might be thinking with awe and reverence of the best things that have been done out of religious conviction, the way faith harnessed effort and resources to monumental achievements: the greatest cathedrals, the music of Bach and Mozart, the poetry of Dante, the novels of Tolstoy, the collective sense of moral destiny and obedience to a higher power. A false, but noble, belief gave rise to all this. Can anything replace that belief, anything that will drive us to the same level of creative grandeur? The rejection of religious conviction is not – he is saying – the end of the matter; it is the start of a much more difficult task: how to rebuild an equally noble outlook, an equally motivating set of beliefs, without relying on the idea of God.

The importance of a belief is different according to whether or not it is true. For example, in a domestic disagreement proving that your partner is wrong might be counterproductive. The belief is not really describing the world, but giving vent to the needs of the person who holds it. So disproving the belief is not in itself much of a help, for the need remains unaddressed. For instance: suppose your partner (or a parent) holds some political views which strike you as naive (to put it gently). They might hold that peace will come to the Middle East when people learn to enjoy each other's cuisine or that the rise of China will bring wisdom to the world. You set yourself to change their mind. You deluge them with facts, you sit up late together watching documentaries, you cut out powerful articles from newspapers and send them links to relevant websites. One possible outcome is that after all this, and some apparent willingness to agree with you, your partner (or parent) simply reverts to their original position: 'I see what you mean, but I still think . . .' Or it may be that they agree but feel sad. Nietzsche would say that their belief was not about how things really are or are likely to be in the world, but rather express the desire that people can learn to understand one another, that enmity can be overcome by small acts of mutual enjoyment – which is a very nice idea, even if it clearly does not apply to geopolitics. Or they may wish that something would bring wisdom to the world (an honourable wish) and they project this onto whatever big theme happens to be around.

In other words, the 'bigger picture' here concerns what a belief is and what a belief is for. Such abstract questions are obviously not our daily fare, but it turns out they are relevant to how we deal with everyday problems, like an argument over the dinner table.

Nietzsche's ideas about religious belief did not arrive fully formed in his mind. He had to work them up from a confused mass of observations, questions to himself, doubts, worries, excited observations. This is inspiration for a notebook: push the idea harder. We could imagine hundreds of little moments for Nietzsche: that guy is a phoney. Why do people have religious faith? What was it like before Christianity came along? Why can't I believe, when lots of intelligent people used to believe (and still do)? Could it be that it used to be different? If I don't accept Christianity, how is it I'm so impressed by Christian art? All these starting points are developed. He does not merely observe and note; he tries to fuse his observations and thoughts into a big-picture thesis.

A similar big-picture thought experiment is conveyed in his slightly bizarre idea of 'eternal recurrence'.

The heaviest burden. What if a demon crept after you one day or night in your loneliest solitude and said to you: 'This life, as you live it now and have lived it, you will have to live again and again, times without number; and there will be nothing new in it, but every pain and every joy and every sigh and all the unspeakably small and great in your life must return to you, and everything in the same series and sequence – and in the same way this spider and this moonlight among the trees, and in the same way this moment and myself. The eternal hourglass of existence will be turned again and again – and you with it, you dust of dust!' – Would you not throw yourself down and gnash your teeth and curse the demon who thus spoke? Or have you experienced a tremendous moment in you in which you would have answered him: 'You are a god and never did I hear anything more divine!' If this thought gained power over you it would, as you are now, transform and perhaps crush you. The question is always: 'Do you want this again and again, times without number?' This lies as the heaviest burden upon all your actions. Or how well disposed towards yourself and towards life would you have to become to have *no greater desire* than for this ultimate eternal sanction and seal.

(*The Gay Science*, 1882)

Lesson: ask yourself, is this thing I am doing worthy of being done again and again? Or am I doing it only for makeshift reasons? Is it a stopgap – or is this how my life really should be?

The point of the thought-experiment is not really to make a claim about what might actually be true. Rather its function is to intensify the sense of the importance and weight of the present moment, so as to counteract our normal tendency to think: I've got lots of time, I'll get serious another day. We can imagine Nietzsche struggling with procrastination, and giving himself orders: Get on with it, treat each moment as precious! And then trying to get this idea to stick in his mind, so that it is always to the fore. He invents a story – with a demon in it.

Or consider another natural frailty: we easily become despondent. We try and try, but are conscious that even though we are proud of our efforts, they really leave so much undone. Envy sets in: others will do better; we will be surpassed. Nietzsche invents for himself an image of heroic failure.

All those brave birds which fly out into the distance, into the farthest distance – it is certain! somewhere or other they will be unable to go on and will perch down on a mast or a bare cliff-face and they will even be thankful for this miserable accommodation! But who could venture to infer from that, that there was *not* an immense open space before them, that they had flown as far as one *could* fly? All our great teachers and predecessors have at last come to a stop; and it will be the same with you and me! But what does that matter to you and me! *Other birds will fly farther!* This insight and faith of ours vies with them in flying up and away; it rises above our heads and above our impotence into the heights and from there surveys the distance and sees before it the flocks of birds which, far stronger than we, still strive whither we have striven, and where everything is sea, sea, sea! – And whither then would we go? Would we *cross* the sea? Whither does this mighty longing draw us, this longing that is worth more to us than any pleasure? Why, just in this direction, to there where all the suns of humanity have hitherto *gone down*? Will it perhaps be said of us one day that we too, *steering westward, hoped to reach an India* – but that it was our fate to be wrecked against infinity?

(*The Gay Science*, 1882)

Yes, you will fail. But you are still an 'aeronaut of the spirit'. Hold onto that name. When you feel envy say: 'But I am an aeronaut of the spirit,' and don't be disheartened.

So much crosses our minds, so much happens but is hard to describe. The journal, diary and notebook are places of hope, in which we long to work out what we think, capture what a day has really meant, define a relationship, memorialize a picnic or an especially wounding row. As you read something strikes you, you underline a striking sentence, scribble in the margin. You press open a new jotter, or find a half-empty page in an old one. But over time, the notes build up. You can't recall quite what it was that struck you, or why it seemed so powerful at the time. The painful fact is that only a few thoughts really stick. If something is to make a difference to our thinking, we probably have to return to it again and again.

A strategy for using Nietzsche is to see him as a balancing agent. He is very insistent on some themes – the need for inner strength, for confronting opposition, for disliking people, for being judgemental – which we tend to downplay. A lot of cultural development over the last several decades has placed a premium on being nice to people, on holding back from strong personal judgement, on avoiding or reducing conflict. And of course there is a great deal to be said in favour of this line of progress. But there is also something to be said against it, and that is often what we hear from Nietzsche. This is the function of an aphorism. Rather than work up a lot of ideas into a big-picture thesis, the aphorism tries to cast a single useful thought in the most abbreviated – and therefore most memorable – form.

One has been a bad spectator of life if one has not also seen the hand that in a considerate fashion – kills.

(Beyond Good and Evil, 1886)

Point: not all the bad things that happen to us come with noise and drama. Such things have happened often. So when they happen to us, it is not a unique curse.

> Under conditions of peace, the warlike man attacks
> himself.
>
> (*Beyond Good and Evil*, 1886)

Point: you will find that you attack yourself, get very self-critical and angry at your own mistakes and missed opportunities. This is not because you are doing anything wrong. It is your strong qualities finding something to do. Give them another and better task – go to war in some way (though not literally, of course).

> One is punished most for one's virtues.
>
> (*Beyond Good and Evil*, 1886)

Point: when people attack us or criticize us, our instinct is to experience this as 'punishment' for our failings, to see it as our fault and therefore as something we deserve. Of course, sometimes that is precisely what is happening. But we must remember that quite often it is good things about us that other people don't like or get frustrated or annoyed by. We must learn to distinguish between these two kinds of attack because they have such different meanings. I can protect my inner sense of self-respect by hanging onto this aphorism.

> One seeks a midwife for his thoughts, another
> someone to whom he can be a midwife: thus origi-
> nates a good conversation.
>
> (*Beyond Good and Evil*, 1886)

Point: we've all had a lot of conversations that, on reflection, did not go very well. And a few that were truly constructive. What went well in those good cases? Sometimes we felt the other person really wanted to help us bring our thoughts to life – a bit like a midwife, really, helping deliver a baby, not a pleasant experience, but incredibly important. So that might explain why some of the best conversations we have had were not especially pleasant – but something important happened in them. Of course, there's no point in having a midwife around if there's no one is labour. So good conversation involves someone needing help, as we have all often done, I suppose, although we did not realize this at the time. We must remember that good conversation has this structure.

Our culture gives a special privilege to the moment of discovery – to the first encounter with an interesting or striking idea. It takes the side of the discoverer, inventor, explorer. But we are generally the users of ideas, so we should put a premium on what makes them stick in our minds. And that's where the aphorism comes in. The point is to be memorable – to be at the front of one's thoughts when the occasion to make use of them arises. That's why repetition is so important, because that is a key mechanism through which ideas get traction in our conduct, which is what we really want.

HOMEWORK

INTRODUCTION
....

You can practise saying 'Nietzsche' by singing along to this video of a clip of the philosophers' drinking song from Monty Python: http://www.youtube.com/watch?v=6QgCfnBtF7M.

The key point is that 'Nietzsche' rhymes with 'teach ya'.

A fine, short overview of the man's philosophy is *Nietzsche* by Michael Tanner, in the Oxford Past Masters series (also called VSI: Very Short Introductions). Tanner is a Cambridge don and *Spectator* music reviewer, who is known in the academic world for his determination not only to know about Nietzsche but to be like him.

I have been influenced by the approach to Nietzsche developed by Lesley Chamberlain, in her charming account of the philosopher's last months of sanity, *Nietzsche in Turin*. She says that her aim is to make friends with him – an idea which applies not only to Nietzsche, of course. The approach of 'making friends with' is my core approach to engaging with big cultural figures.

When Nietzsche Wept (2007), a film directed by Pinchas Perry, imagines Nietzsche taking a 'talking cure' with Josef Breuer (an early colleague of Freud). There is something slightly amateurish about the film, but it provides a charming way of entering the cultural environment of the time – and there is a good early sequence of Nietzsche lecturing in an almost empty auditorium. In it he is portrayed as very difficult to like.

1

HOW TO FIND YOUR BEST SELF

....

The musical work *Delius: A Mass of Life* (1905) is a majestic and expansive response, not so much to the precise ideas of Nietzsche, but to a sense of wondrous human adventure and nobility.

2

ON VISITING THE PYRAMIDS

....

Compare Nietzsche's question 'What might you need the pyramids for?' with the more standard approach, exemplified by the reviews on Tripadvisor, which lays out the basics:

Type: Ancient Ruins, Landmarks/ Points of Interest, Historic Sites, Monuments/ Statues
Activities: Horse riding, Dining

> **Description:** Perhaps the most recognizable among the Seven Wonders of the World; the exact origin of these majestic pyramids continues to spark debate.
> http://www.tripadvisor.com.au/Attraction_Review-g294202-d317746-Reviews-Pyramids_of_Giza-Giza_Giza_Governorate.html

This implies the kinds of demand that (conceivably) could lead someone to the outskirts of Cairo: 'My interests are dining, ancient monuments and horse riding. Is there a place I can do all three?' Or: 'I'd like to see one of the Seven Wonders of the Ancient World, but I'm worried I might not recognize it when I get there. Can you direct me to the most recognizable of them?'

Nietzscheadvisor might carry the following:

> **Type:** Ancient Ruins, Landmarks/ Points of Interest, Historic Sites, Monuments/ Statues
> **Activities:** Either encouragement in great endeavour or ant-like crawling
> **Description:** Perhaps the supreme monuments to aristocratic disdain, these majestic pyramids are immensely popular with democratic tourists – a contradiction that continues to not spark debate.

3

DEALING WITH CONFLICT

....

The most impressive statue of Apollo (though it is actually a Roman copy of a lost Greek original) is the Apollo Belvedere in the Vatican Museum: http://mv.vatican.va/3_EN/pages/x-Schede/MPCs/MPCs_Sala02_01.html

4

THE TROUBLED PATH TO FREEDOM AND MATURITY

....

The final chapter of Alain de Botton's *Consolations of Philosophy* (2001) provides an intriguing analysis of Nietzsche's attitude to achievement, which I have drawn on.

In 1899, in his last few months of life, Nietzsche was filmed sitting in a chair. Nothing happens. *Nietzsche – 'Last Days' Footage – 1899* is on YouTube: http://www.youtube.com/watch?v=Fzp7iCaWNvE. Is it haunting or boring? I can't make up my mind.

5

ON CHANGING ONE'S MIND

....

Nietzsche has an intriguing, though brief, role in Tony Palmer's monumental biopic *Wagner*, with Richard Burton in the lead role and Ronald Pickup as Nietzsche.

The philosopher's love–hate relationship with the great composer is finely portrayed. *Wagner* (1983) is at the Internet Movie Database.

6
THE MERITS OF SHOCK THERAPY
·········

The heroic aspect of Nietzsche is powerfully expressed in the 'tone poem' by Richard Strauss, *Also Sprach Zarathustra* (a musical interpretation, composed in 1896, of Nietzsche's book). The dramatic, and very famous, opening section was used to great effect in Stanley Kubrick's *2001: A Space Odyssey*.

Christopher Hamilton's book *Middle Age* (2009) uses Nietzsche in a dramatic and intense exploration of the meaning of the author's own life. But more than the specific references, this book is written throughout in a spirit that is deeply influenced by Nietzsche.

Nietzsche's concern with sternness finds a fascinating echo in aspects of *Battle Hymn of the Tiger Mother* by Amy Chua, published in 2011. It explores a style of parenting which sets high ambitious goals and insists that the child attain them – an attitude which was profoundly shocking to many readers. But the success of the book suggests that there is wide recognition that she is onto something.

The importance of facing, rather than avoiding, fear is summed up in the perfect title of the late Susan Jeffers' book *Feel the Fear and Do It Anyway* (1987).

7
BE A NOBLE NOT A SLAVE

....

The Three Musketeers and its several sequels by Alexandre Dumas were written before Nietzsche developed his philosophical views. The characters of d'Artagnan and Porthos (less Athos, in that book, and Aramis) flesh out the brave, energetic, happy, self-loving, despising attitudes that Nietzsche sketches. A nice Nietzschean touch is that the great enemy of the first book, Cardinal Richelieu, later becomes the Musketeers' patron, and although they finally oppose him they never despise him.

The character of Gollum in *The Hobbit* and *The Lord of the Rings* is in some ways a case study of *ressentiment*; he is unable ever to comprehend the decency of Frodo and hates Frodo more when he is generous towards him.

8
DON'T PULL YOUR PUNCHES

....

Women Who Love Too Much (2004) by Robin Norwood looks in more detail at the problem of not admitting that another person is causing you grave trouble. Because being nice is such an achievement, decent people are prone to being *too* nice. Nietzsche offers some strong advice in the opposite direction.

CONCLUSION: ON KEEPING A NOTEBOOK

....

The theme of a god who dies – or is killed – was memorably explored in Sir James George Frazer's classic study of myth *The Golden Bough* (1890). Nietzsche's aim is to reconsider Christianity as a human cultural achievement, rather than as a final revelation of the spiritual order of reality.

ACKNOWLEDGEMENTS

....

I'm deeply grateful to the friends – especially Christopher Hamilton – who, over the years, have introduced me to Nietzsche's work and thought, although I'm conscious that I have taken from him something rather different from what they had hoped. When you try to make an author's writing your own it's inevitable that it gets reshaped by your own preoccupations.

As an adolescent, I occasionally heard Nietzsche's name round the family dinner table. I'd like to thank my parents for fostering an attitude to books and ideas, which I now realize is not to be taken for granted. They were – and still are – always searching for personal import: why does an idea matter to you, how does it change your life?

Helen, William, Charlotte and Pippi have become highly skilled at teasing me for my excessively earnest attitudes. I don't always take it well, but I know they are wise: I'd like to offer in print the gratitude which I do not adequately express in real life.

And, finally, special thanks to all the people at The School of Life and Pan Macmillan who have made working on this book such a pleasure.

A note on the extracts used throughout this book:

Because they are pulled from large works, which discuss diverse themes, the extracts have occasionally been lightly edited to allow a particular line of thought to emerge more cleanly. Most are out of copyright but I'd like to credit the following:

On the Genealogy of Morals, translated by Walter Kaufmann and R. J. Hollingdale, Vintage Books (1967).
  Also available as a free online source:
  http://nietzsche.holtof.com/Nietzsche_on_the_genealogy_of_morals/on_the_genealogy_of_morals.htm.
  And archived at The Nietzsche Channel.

The Birth of Tragedy and The Case of Wagner, translated by Walter Kaufmann, Vintage Books (1967).
  Also available as a free online source:
  http://www.davemckay.co.uk/philosophy/nietzsche/nietzsche.php?name=nietzsche.1872.birthoftragedy.kaufmann.index.

The Gay Science, translated by Walter Kaufmann, Vintage Books (1974).
  Also available as a free online source:
  http://archive.org/stream/Nietzsche-TheGay-Science/Nietzsche-GaySciencewk_djvu.txt.